REFLECTED WISDOM

A COLLECTION OF ESSAYS

JAMES V. LEE

Foreward by Tom Ziglar, Proud Son of Zig Ziglar

James V. Lee

Reflected Wisdom
A Collection of Essays

Copyright © 2010 by James V. Lee

ISBN: 0-9663870-8-7
ISBN:978-0-9663870-8-7

Library of Congress Control Number: 2010914836

Published in the United States by Salado Press, LLC

SALADO PRESS

P. O. Box 852011

Richardson, Texas 75085-2011

This book is dedicated to my wife, Hazel Juanita Lee,
September 25, 1929 – January 6, 2010

Whatever principles the reader may find in this book, were complemented, embellished, or maybe even originated by my wife of sixty years, an elegant, classy lady. I really don't know how those qualities were inculcated into her from the time she was a little girl. She grew up in the same rural hardscrabble conditions in West Texas that I did. I guess her sweet elegance is the reason I fell in love with her. From the beginning, we believed that God was at the heart of our union, and so we were utterly committed to one another. Her courage during the lingering illness of her last six years was a source of inspiration to everyone who knew her.

Acknowledgement

Although I taught essay writing aboard U.S. Navy ships for Central Texas College for five years, I didn't get serious about actually writing essays until Michael Landauer, an assistant editorial page editor, of *The Dallas Morning News*, invited me to write an occasional opinion piece for that newspaper, beginning in 2006. Michael critiqued the twenty essays in this book that originally appeared in *The Dallas Morning News*. As a professional, he saw my work through different eyes and frequently suggested constructive changes. I owe my thanks to him for improving my modest skills. He has not read my here-to-fore unpublished essays. So he is taking a leap of faith that I won't embarrass him.

That which has been is what will be,
That which is done is what will be done,
And there is nothing new under the sun.
Is there anything of which it may be said,
"See, this is new"?

It has already been in ancient times before us.
There is no remembrance of former things,
Nor will there be any remembrance of things that
are to come
By those who will come after.

Ecclesiastes 1:9-11 (NKJ)

About the Book

A friend once told me, "If we both agreed on everything, one of us would be nuts." Thus, it is not my expectation or objective that all readers of this book be in total agreement with what I have written. Rather, my objective is to stimulate in the reader the incentive to think for himself and rely upon available facts to arrive at improved enlightenment. "As iron sharpens iron, so one person sharpens another." Proverbs 27:17 (NIV) A nation led by honest, informed thinkers has little to fear from destructive ideologies.

No claim is made for any original idea. Everything that follows already has been expressed in different words somewhere by someone with greater scholarship and insight. What does follow is an attempt to formulate fundamental truths in concise, thoughtful entertainment on subjects of universal interest.

Wise old heads have always said that wisdom is wasted on youth. One of my friends expressed it somewhat indelicately by saying that, "Every generation has to learn firsthand the folly of skinning a skunk." It's my sincere hope that readers of all ages of these essays can avoid a few skunks.

James V. Lee

Essays may be expressed in ten different forms.
This book attempts to illustrate each form.

Contents

Foreward

I enjoyed reading James Lee's collection of essays. In it he shares some very interesting history from his personal perspective, reflecting the cultural mores of a time few Americans will recall but all should reflect upon. Many of the articles are thought-provoking, steeped in common sense and sound life principles. The reading is easy, pleasant and meaningful. Aptly titled *Reflected Wisdom*, it's a book I recommend to all. I believe it holds a particular value and interest for parents for their young adult children.

Tom Ziglar, Proud Son of Zig Ziglar

NARRATION

Return to OK

This essay first appeared in The Dallas Morning News *on August 17, 2006.*

Some time ago, I attended a gathering of some folks who used to make up the OK community in the Texas Panhandle. For me, it was a pilgrimage to rediscover my roots.

In this part of the Texas Plains where cotton is king, I discovered that my roots had been plowed up. Even though the intervening years had changed the people in attendance, I still recognized many of them. But not the land.

Nothing but a dead tree remained of the old Tucker place where I was born about four miles southwest of O'Donnell, Texas. A cotton field now stretches to the horizon where the OK School stood. At Grandview

Lee with Aunt Alice Greenlee at Lee Birth Place

3

School, where I spent my first school year, sat a lone fertilizer tank. And nothing remained to remind me of several metal-roofed shacks I had called home.

Although I left when I was still a child, the OK community was the mold that formed the man that I became. Located on U.S. Highway 87 about a mile east of OK School on a slight knoll rising out of the flat terrain, a four-room structure housed my grandparents, five uncles, one aunt, my mother and me, a first-grader.

Actually, it was two two-room houses placed side by side to form an L shape. The house was of single-wall construction formed by 1-by-12 planks with 1-by-4 strips nailed over the cracks, the "insulation" being heavy wallpaper nailed on with metal buttons.

The room adjoining the kitchen doubled as a living room and as a bedroom for my grandparents. Here, by an oil lamp, my grandfather would read stories to the three youngest of the clan. The unheated boys' room had a northwest exposure, and during a blue norther, it had to be one of the coldest places on earth.

Social activity on cool summer nights and warm Sunday afternoons centered on an east-facing porch where the women in the family somehow kept the family in reasonably clean clothes with a rub board, lye soap, and water heated in an iron kettle in the yard. Our version of running water was to run a wagon and team of horses to a water well about a mile away and haul the water back in 55-gallon barrels.

These were the Great Depression years in West Texas, and home on the range was rapidly becoming home on the farm as vast stretches of prairie flowers surrendered to the plow. My family started out as tenant farmers. The land gave us an opportunity. That was all we had. That was all we needed. I was taught that the best place to find a helping hand was at the end of my own arm. I learned by example. We picked cotton right alongside migrants. Everybody got paid according to what he or she could produce. It was an equal opportunity. That this kind of work might have been beneath our dignity never entered the conversation at the supper table.

Community activity revolved around the OK schoolhouse, which got its name from the initials of an old cowboy. Just how the school came to be named after him is still unknown to me. But having a brick exterior, it was an imposing structure compared to the other buildings of rural West Texas. Facing prevailing southerly winds, wide front steps led to the auditorium that became a Baptist church on Sundays.

In the absence of radio or TV, the OK community relied upon the very gifted musical talent of several families for entertainment frequently performed on this stage. This was long before country and western music became obsessed with drunkenness and adultery, which never would have been accepted on the stage of the OK School.

Like the relics of this Prohibition era, no evidence of OK exists, except in the minds of its dwindling survivors. In spite of our shoestring beginnings, probably all of us now have far more creature comforts than we expected.

Since leaving OK, I have traveled to 40 countries, more than 20 islands, most of the states, and on almost every ocean of the world. But no place has had a greater influence on me than the scene of my formative years. The eyes, voices, and handshakes of all the people who returned for the reunion still reflect the spirit of hard work, independence, integrity and friendship that characterized the community during the Great Depression.

These are my real roots, and I'm grateful to those who nurtured them.

Rural Texas Culture

When I graduated from high school at Ackerly, Texas, in 1943, the town had a population of about 300 people, which probably swelled to about 350 when Hispanics from South Texas and Mexico showed up during the cotton-picking season. So the community, including the area within twenty miles in any direction, lacked the resources to be much of a cultural center in West Texas.

Even though surrounding farms contributed enough kids to the school system to maintain twelve grades, a six-man football team, and a basketball team, all culture was homegrown and performed on the stage of the auditorium of the elementary school. The entire student body assembled here on December 8, 1941 to hear President Roosevelt make his famous "Day of Infamy" speech about the Japanese attack on Pearl Harbor the preceding day. Even though a high school junior, I had never heard of Pearl Harbor, and hearing the president ask congress to declare war against Japan and its allies in Europe sobered me into realizing that I would eventually wear a military uniform.

Usually the auditorium served less auspicious purposes. However, every graduating class did become the object of pomp and circumstance while stately marching down the aisle to the same tune played on a piano year after year.

Sometimes the math teacher showed 16mm movies on Saturday nights, which always included his fresh popped popcorn. And the English teacher formed a group of high school girls into an ensemble that sang in three part harmony. We thought they were good. One of the elementary teachers thought up the idea of a rhythm band for some of the elementary students. Keeping time to a piano with blocks of wood, triangles, and other noise makers struck me as something that would never catch on. Occasionally, talented adults in the community performed skits or musical entertainment.

The main cultural school event was a three-act play performed by the high school students. The most memorable play was a melodrama in which I played the part of a character called Bluebeard Bronson, an ax murderer. The stage set included a closet whose interior was exposed to the audience when the door was opened. The cardboard back of the closet had a hole in a section through which a girl thrust her head with some of her blonde hair twisted around a nail above her head. Red paint splattered on the wall beneath her head completed the illusion that her head was cut off and hanging by her hair in the closet. At a very dramatic moment, one of the characters in the play opened the door to the terrified screams of all the little kids sitting on the front row.

At the climax of the play, I was holding some other characters at bay with a pistol. Slipping up behind me and jabbing a gun into my ribs, the play's hero was supposed to speak the line: "Drop that gun, or I'll pulverize your liver!" But all during rehearsals, he kept clowning around and saying, "...I'll fertilize your liver!" So what did he say on our big night when all the mothers and daddies and everybody else in the community filled the auditorium? It was the only funny line in the entire play.

I'm not aware of any ex-students from Ackerly that ever made it big on stage or screen, but up the road a piece at O'Donnell a fellow named Dan Blocker gained fame as Hoss Cartwright in the TV series Bonanza. I reckon it's ok for Ackerly folks to borrow some of Dan's luster and claim him as just one of us good ole West Texas boys.

Mom Made an Offer too Good to Refuse

This essay first appeared in The Dallas Morning News *on January 24, 1998.*

One of the main issues in the ongoing tobacco controversy is keeping the stuff out of the hands of children. When I was 11 years old, my mother and dad had split up, and I was sent from the farm to live for a year with my grandparents in Lubbock, Texas, a city viewed by my mother as a great metropolis of 30,000 people awash in sin and iniquity. Her concept of this evil influence partly originated in the smoking and drinking habits of my grandfather. I got my first taste of whiskey when I was sick, and he made a whiskey toddy for me. I regarded it the same as foul-tasting medicine.

My introduction to cigarettes was more adventuresome. In those days, "ready rolls" were a luxury. To save money, many smokers bought tobacco by the sack or can and rolled their own cigarettes. The neighborhood gang I hung out with in Lubbock devised an even more economical plan. We picked up cigarette butts off the street, the sidewalk and wherever else we could find them. Then we split them open and put the tobacco in a can. After that, someone got some cigarette papers from the store, and we rolled our own. It wasn't the thought of picking up somebody's tuberculosis or some other horrible disease that turned me against cigarettes. It was the foul taste. And I still don't know why that initial foul taste doesn't offend all young senses.

Not knowing about my introduction to these two vices, my mother approached the issue head-on. She appealed to my greed. She came to town one day and, taking me aside said, "Jamie, if you won't drink until you are 21, I'll give you $10. And if you don't smoke until you are 21, I'll give you another $10." Payday was to be on my 21st birthday. Even at age 11, I recognized this as a no-brainer. Since I already was repulsed by both vices, I can't claim any moral superiority.

So the money was just the frosting. However, it held out more appeal than you might think. Twenty dollars isn't much money today, but let me tell you what $20 meant to me in 1938. I used to spend some of my summers with my uncle and aunt just south of O'Donnell in the Texas Panhandle. Uncle Earl paid me five cents a row to hoe cotton. The fields were laid out in quarter sections, so each row was a half-mile long. I was a pretty industrious kid and could hoe 20 rows a day. That's 10 miles of hoeing to earn $1. So, to me, $20 was tantamount to hoeing a row of cotton 200 miles long. Now, I sometimes wonder what would happen if anybody who wanted to drink and smoke had to first clear the weeds off a strip of land 42 inches wide stretching from Dallas, Texas, to Shreveport, Louisiana. More than likely, the nation would incur a severe shortage of drinkers and smokers.

By the time I was 21, my mother had forgotten all about our deal. Because of the many splendid deeds she did for me, I never reminded her. Cigarettes and liquor never tempted me, but what my mother didn't know, and never did find out, was that I could out-cuss any kid in the neighborhood.

Getting Religion

My grandfather was a paradox. Although possessed of a few moral faults, he was a hard working and respected businessman in the small West Texas community of OK where he served on the school board. On some Lord's Days, he would load up the youngest of the clan in his Model A Ford sedan and take us to the OK school house that served as the church on Sunday. Very likely he would invite the preacher home for the noon meal. Here I was introduced to Christianity.

Each time I went to Sunday school, I got a little card with a picture with a fragment of a verse of scripture, such as "...even as the Father has said unto me so I speak." I still have a two-inch stack of those little cards, attesting to my faithful attendance. I enjoyed Sunday school and I'm sure it reinforced the moral values

Sunday School Card

that my mother was trying to inculcate into me.

When my grandparents moved to Lubbock, I moved with them since my mother was a single mom and times were tough. I attended my fourth and sixth grades in Lubbock schools. Strangely, even though I was drawn to Sunday school teachings, it was here that I started to use cuss words. I picked that up from my grandfather. I guess you could say he was bilingual, since he spoke fluent profanity. Fortunately, my strait laced mother never did find out about how well I excelled in this character flaw.

Following my fourth-grade year, my mother remarried and I went to live with her and my new dad at Ackerly, Texas, where I spent my fifth grade. But then the school district around Ackerly was changed so that I would have to attend a one-room school on a nearby ranch. So I was sent back to Lubbock for my sixth-grade year.

Then the school districts around Ackerly were again realigned so that I could attend school at Ackerly where I spent the rest of my school years, except for my sophomore year at Sparenburg, Texas.

My best friend Grady Reese and his family were members of the Church of Christ and I began to lean in that direction. Then some summers after the crops had been laid by, Harvey Childress, a preacher from Ogden, Utah, would hold two-week revival meetings. Everybody in and around

Ackerly liked Harvey. He not only packed the simple, frame church building every night, but people sat in their cars around the building and listened through the open windows.

On the last Sunday of the meeting, our noon meal was "dinner on the ground." Temporary out-door tables were fashioned by laying long boards across saw horses on which women of the church would place their food that they had prepared at home. On such occasions, flies were a consider-able nuisance, so some of the women would po-sition themselves along the tables and wave dish towels to keep the flies from the food while other people ate. Following the meal, we would sing all afternoon as the old men in the amen corner patted their feet on the church building's wooden floor to the time of the a cappella singing. The song service would end in time for all the farmers to return home to milk and feed their cows before returning for the evening preaching service.

That's about the time I was baptized and my best friend and I drilled each other in learning the books of the Bible. We also memorized a considerable number of verses in the Bible. We dreamed great dreams. Grady was going to do the preaching, while I was going to lead singing at revival meetings, and we were going to con-vert the world. We both ended up in the navy in WWII and were roommates for one semester at Abilene Christian College (now University). Our relationship since has been reduced to exchanging Christmas cards and occasional emails.

One thing that Harvey said in one of his sermons hit a very responsive chord with me. I can still picture him quoting Phil. 4:8. "Finally brethren, whatever things are true, whatever things are noble, whatever things are just, whatever things are pure, whatever things are lovely, whatever things are of good report, if there be any virtue, if there be any praise, think about these things." And I made a profound discovery. I often drove a tractor from sunup to sundown and still had cows to feed and milk before eating supper and dropping dog tired into bed after a bath in a number two wash tub.

Lee Driving a Tractor

Then one day while driving the tractor, I got to thinking about verses of scripture and just meditating along spiritual lines. I noticed that when I drove in from the field, I really didn't feel very tired. That was the beginning of my understanding of the Proverb that says, "As a man thinks in his heart, so is he." Much has been written about the effect of thought processes on a person's body. I had this partially figured out at about age 14.

Subsequently, some ministers exposed me to some ideas that I knew went beyond the teachings of scripture. I heard any number of sermons on the imperative of total abstinence from alcoholic drinks. Since Jesus had turned water into wine at a wedding, I wondered if the preacher thought He was a bootlegger. I also wondered what else he might be wrong about. I knew that the scriptures condemned both drunkenness and gluttony. But strangely, I never heard gluttony condemned from any pulpit. I learned to be a skeptical listener, and if what I heard from the pulpit didn't square with the scripture, I just didn't let it bother me. It's been my heart's desire to grow spiritually over the years and be a wholesome influence on other people. Only God knows how that has worked out.

Reflected Wisdom

Cattle Baron

While I was living with my grandparents during my sixth grade at Lubbock, Texas, my grandfather took two of my young uncles and me to his farm near Levelland, Texas, that an older uncle was tenant farming. One uncle was my senior by eight months and the other a little over three years. My grandfather had some whiteface heifers in a pen and told us we could pick out one to keep. My uncles sold their calves almost immediately and spent the money. I had a different vision. This heifer would be the beginning of a vast herd that I would own some day.

When that school year ended, my dad and I went out to the farm to claim my calf. But my beautiful whiteface calf had turned into an ugly black hornless beast! Although I was greatly disappointed, I didn't say anything about the switch, since the calf was a gift anyway. I don't know whether it was my grandfather or my uncle who switched calves.

As soon as the heifer was old enough, we mated her to a fine whiteface bull. But when she gave birth, she lay on the newborn calf and killed it. So I sold her and bought another cow that was mostly Guernsey. Before she gave birth to her first calf, my dad had a Jersey that gave birth to twins. I saw this as my chance to make up for lost time by owning a twin-bearing cow! So I persuaded my dad to trade cows with me. It wasn't long before the Guernsey gave birth to her calf, but it would be another nine months before the Jersey gave birth again.

Meanwhile, I had finished high school and needed money for college expenses at Texas Tech. I sold the Jersey for the exact amount of my first semester's tuition.

Although this little episode disappointed me at the time, it served me well in later years. As a thirteen-year-old kid, I assumed that my family would deal with me fairly out of love and protect me from my own poor judgment. For whatever reason, they chose not to. So I learned early on that a deal is a deal, even if it's bad deal, and that my word is my bond. That measure of integrity became permanently entrenched in my character and also taught me to thoughtfully evaluate potential problems before making serious decisions. However, some unfortunate cases of misplaced trust over the years presented a sobering reminder of this childhood lesson that, in addition, instilled in me a determination not to take advantage of other people who also may be vulnerable by their own naiveté. I guess this was my introduction to the principle, "love people and use things," not "love things and use people."

James V. Lee

Pacific Pleasure Cruise

This essay first appeared in The Dallas Morning News *on July 2, 2007.*

Tom Brokhaw set off a flood of military stories when he wrote *The Greatest Generation*. Heroic exploits seem to be the norm of these books. Although time embellishes facts for all of us, most of the stories probably are essentially true. I have two books in print about these heroes.

But for some of us World War II types, "hero" is more of a word in the dictionary than a reality. Volunteering at age 17 for naval service in late 1944, I spent my WWII naval career mostly in training or at some receiving station waiting for a permanent assignment. Following boot camp in San Diego, the Navy sent me to quartermaster school in Gulfport, Mississippi.

During my training in quartermaster school, one night I was assigned to guard a portion of the fence that surrounded the naval base. Since WWII was in full fury, I was charged to protect this segment of the United States against all enemies, both foreign and domestic. My weaponry for this important mission was a dummy wooden rifle and a plastic bayonet. Thus armed, I was not to allow anyone to come through the fence.

My hours of boredom quickly turned to full alert when I detected someone attempting to enter this secure compound. "Halt!" I firmly commanded the intruder. He didn't halt. Emerging through the fence, a somewhat disheveled and disoriented young man presented himself. He seemed, as we swabbies were wont to say, about three sheets to the wind. Obviously lost, he was thankful to remain with me until the patrol officer made his next round in his Jeep. Word spread quickly through my company that I was a hero. I had captured a highly decorated Army Air Corps officer.

While there, the war in Europe ended on May 8, 1945. Then, while I was temporarily located in a receiving station on the West Coast, presumably waiting for a ship to take me to the anticipated invasion of Japan, the second atom bomb exploded over Japan on Aug. 9, 1945, effectively ending the Pacific war.

Shortly afterward, I shipped out on a destroyer to a receiving station in Hawaii, where I played chess and drank pineapple juice for some weeks before boarding the USS *Kwajalein*, a baby flat top, to Guam. En route, we ran into a typhoon

USS LST 930 *at Hollandia, New Guinea*

that old sailors still talk about. The storm broke the moorings on one of the torpedo bombers on the flight deck, flipping it upside down on two small observation planes, which were off loaded in cargo nets in Guam.

After four months in Guam—where I spent my spare time swimming and collecting shells off a coral reef, or just hanging out wherever I could stay out of trouble—I finally got a permanent assignment to *LST 930*, a big, amphibious landing ship. It had made the landings at Iwo Jima and Okinawa. Some of the crew saw the Marines raise the flag over Mt. Suribachi.

Japanese POWs at Saipan

The entire port side on the second deck was set up as operating compartments and medical aid stations. Doctors and corpsmen patched up countless soldiers and marines right off the beach before transferring them to a hospital ship farther offshore.

My time on the ship was spent on a trip to Milne Bay, New Guinea, where we loaded up surplus war materiel to transfer to Hollandia, New Guinea. Then it was back to Saipan, back to Guam, back to Hawaii, back to San Francisco. We were towed about half the distance from Guam to Hawaii. Both engines just quit.

During a night watch right after I boarded that

New Guinea Village, Lee Next to Children

old tub, a fire broke out in the No. 3 generator. We were the lead ship in a three-ship convoy doing 10 knots. The captain on the control tower yelled down the voice tube to cut our speed to five knots and for me to turn on the breakdown lights to alert the ships behind us. The aft bulkhead in the wheelhouse was replete with switches. I couldn't find the "breakdown switch" because it was labeled by another name.

While I frantically searched for the switch, anger filled the captain's repeated commands, bellowed in colorful Navalese. After a few admonitions from the captain to get the "G-D" lights on, someone roused the second-class quartermaster out of his rack to flip the switch. Meanwhile, the captain had to turn the ship out of formation to keep from being rammed. He was not pleased and called me up to the control tower after the crisis was over to pass that sentiment on to me in rather frank, threatening language. I think that was my most memorable experience during my South Pacific pleasure cruise, or maybe my entire naval career.

I stayed aboard to help decommission the ship at San Francisco and was promoted to QM 3/C. Not sure why. But I earned $75 a month for three weeks.

It's my ambition to be the last surviving veteran of World War II. The young journalist who will interview me is going to be so disappointed.

James V. Lee

What Might Have Been

This essay first appeared in The Dallas Morning News *on September 7, 2007.*

Now that I'm an octogenarian, I get unsolicited hugs from 81-year-old women who wouldn't have given me the time of day when they were 18. I asked my wife about that, and she said, "Well, they don't see you as a threat any more."

Somehow I don't feel complimented. What has diminished about me that formerly posed a threat to women? I really don't want an answer to that question, but how could I have been a threat during all those years—and not know it?

I don't recall ever making a deliberate choice to be either a threat or non-threat to anybody. Probably, most of my life's choices met quick oblivion. The power of choice is the foundation of all other power with its attendant consequences. It's the only thing that human beings truly possess.

Young people often blithely make poor choices and give no thought to the consequences. That's why wise old heads have always said that youth is wasted on the young—the same wise old heads who blithely made poor choices themselves.

John Greenleaf Whittier penned these words in his poem "Maude Muller:"

For of all sad words of tongue or pen, the saddest are these: 'It might have been!'

But that's not necessarily true. At least one "might have been" may have allowed me to dodge a bullet—literally. As a young man, I seriously considered a career with the FBI. Those were the J. Edgar Hoover years, when a communist lurked under every rock. The TV show *I was a Communist for the FBI* enjoyed popular weekly programming. My wife convinced me that my face is an open book, and that I couldn't lie well enough to avoid getting shot.

She thwarted my plans to be a U.S. Air Force pilot, too. Having set an Air Force record for coordination and having perfect hearing and vision, I would have finished flight training in time to become a combat ace in the Korean War—or a casualty face-down in a Korean rice paddy.

Another major choice occurred during our last year in college. She required an appendectomy right after we had broken off our 15-month engagement. Visiting her in the hospital seemed the decent thing to do. As they say, the rest is history.

I choose to put an optimistic spin on most matters. I probably would have done well as an FBI agent, and basking in the glow of Washington dignitaries would have been a rush. The downside would have been uncontrollable absences from my family.

Flying supersonic jets is a dangerous business, but I assume it would have been the other guy that crashed and burned, and I would have retired as an Air Force general.

Regarding that appendectomy, it's been said that a marriage is made in heaven, but isn't it an accident of geography? Or did God, knowing that I am soft touch, arrange for that operation? I know I could have made some other woman a good husband, but I don't waste time fantasizing about it.

Actually, I'm incapable of fantasizing about life without Nita. I love my kids, warts and all, and believe they are superior to any that would have been borne by a different woman.

As a nation of free people, it's fashionable to think that we are blessed with sound judgment leading to judicious decisions. But investment experts say that some people will spend more time and thought on their grocery list than they do on a stock purchase.

I know for certain that my own life has taken major twists and turns brought about by nothing more than a sentence or two from someone I scarcely knew. For example, in 1989, a man I had just met handed me a slip of paper saying, "If you don't mind traveling, call this number in Norfolk, Virginia."

For the next five years, I had a front-row seat to the world teaching writing aboard U.S. Navy ships at sea for Central Texas College. My 16 deployments on 13 different ships was the adventure of a lifetime.

But, even before all that traveling, I guess I had always occupied a front-row seat to the world and was unaware of it—just as I was oblivious of my threat to women.

DESCRIPTION

Beyond Words

This essay first appeared in The Dallas Morning News *on November 10, 2006.*

Tomorrow is Veterans' Day, formerly known as Armistice Day—the time when the Allies and the Central Powers agreed to end World War I at 11:11 a.m. on Nov. 11, 1918, in a railroad car in a French forest. Express appreciation for their sacrifice by buying a red poppy from some veteran. You see, following WWI, red poppies bloomed extensively over formerly blood-soaked Belgium and French battlefields and were immortalized in John McCrae's poem "In Flanders Field," which begins, "In Flanders Fields the poppies blow/Between the crosses, row on row..."

Now, disabled veterans from all wars assemble the paper poppies to raise funds for their rehabilitation and other veterans' issues.

A few years ago, my wife and I got up close and personal to what the WWI soldiers went through. Verdun, France, likely is not on the itinerary of most American tourists. But going to Verdun was a pilgrimage for my wife Nita because her father was gassed and wounded there in WWI.

Verdun isn't just a place. It's an experience. No words or pictures can adequately describe the spirit of the area and the overwhelming emotions that torment the visitor. Verdun is a beautiful city, but somehow it still seems to reek with horror and death. The hills, once denuded by endless shellfire, are reforested. Yet neither trees nor grass can hide the ugly pockmarks of explosions or the outlines of abandoned trenches.

We took a taxi to the American sector to see the names of the Red Diamond Division on the huge Montfaucon monument overlooking a field of endless crosses. The day was overcast, and rain began to drizzle just as we stepped out of the taxi to approach the monument, which housed a chapel. How symbolic! In the fall of 1918, much of this area was a quagmire. Because of the constant shelling and rain, mud descended as much as 30 feet.

The United States committed 1 million men to the war, and more than 100,000 became casualties, including Nita's father. The fighting pulverized more than a dozen villages and thousands of men out of existence, their final resting place "known only to God."

Three gaping craters marked the former village of Fleury. The very air seemed to be the breath of a million ghosts. The hardships of the men who fought there were complete. The rain, the mud, the stench of dead bodies, the stench of human waste—these alone were sufficient for perfect misery. But added to that were the terror of poison gas, hand-to-hand combat and constant shelling of heavy artillery, which gave a new description to survivors: shell-shocked. Yet they fought, bled, died—and won. Neither Nita nor I are prone to tears, but neither of us could contain them.

As a final gesture before entering a taxi to leave the memorial, she gathered a few poppies from the roadside. They rest in a lovely frame on our wall as a permanent memorial.

Haruka

This essay first appeared in The Dallas Morning News *on March 9, 2007.*

A small clay bell dangling from a pale blue cord encased in a glass bell jar sits on my book shelf with other memorabilia. It's a popular Japanese good luck charm to drive away evil spirits. How I acquired it is a story that still astonishes me.

My visit to the shrines at Kamakura, Japan, in 1990 when I was a college professor assigned to U.S. Navy ships began with an unforgettable encounter. As I stepped off the train at Hase Station, I puzzled over a map trying to decide which way to turn. An attractive, well-dressed young woman who had also disembarked approached me and indicated she wanted to look at my map that showed the locations of the shrines in both English and Japanese. After I pointed out where I wanted to go, she smiled and motioned for me to follow her.

Although we didn't speak each other's language, Haruka and I managed to exchange names. Walking briskly, we arrived at Hasedara, the first shrine on my list. Here, she began a series of surprises. There was a small admission fee, which I attempted to pay for both of us, but she insisted on buying her own ticket.

Being a Christian, I viewed this shrine and the ones to follow as mere interesting curiosities, but out of respect for Haruka's belief, I quietly observed and followed her lead in everything she did with the hope of acquiring a more enlightened understanding of the Japanese culture. Subsequently, another Japanese lady told me that the religion of most Japanese is a mixture of polytheistic Shintoism, the worship of gods in nature, and Buddhism, the philosophy of Buddha who is revered as the model of a fully enlightened person. These religions have priests, but they are only called into use for deaths, weddings or trouble of some sort.

Outside the main building that housed the eleven-headed Hase Kannon, the goddess of mercy, Haruka purchased a flower arrangement and placed it before a small shrine already bedecked with several bouquets. Next, she clapped her hands and assumed a standing prayer posture before another small edifice where coins were deposited through slats. After watching her deposit a coin, I started to follow suit with one of mine. She stopped me and insisted that I deposit one of hers. By this ritual the Japanese ask the goddess to make their wishes come true. Typical requests include good health, world peace and passing school exams.

Then she turned to a large, brass incense burner and placed her face in the vapors, all the time smiling and using her hands to concentrate the smoke around her body. The vapors are credited with providing such qualities as good health, pretty faces or smarter children.

When Haruka completed this ritual, she took me inside the temple where she again stood quietly in prayer before this ornate, 30-foot image. Leaving there we went outside to see the magnificent view of the Miura Peninsula, where she used my camera to take my picture and then motioned for me to take her picture. Outside the temple, a table displayed some souvenirs where I tried to buy some postcards. Again she stopped me, indicating that I should get them at the next shrine, the Great Buddha. But before leaving the table of souvenirs, she bought the little spherical clay bell attached to a pale blue cord. In retrospect, I know it was her expression of kindness toward me.

Next, we walked rapidly to the Great Buddha. Immediately inside the grounds was a covered fountain with several long-handled dippers. Taking one of the dippers, she poured water over my hands and then

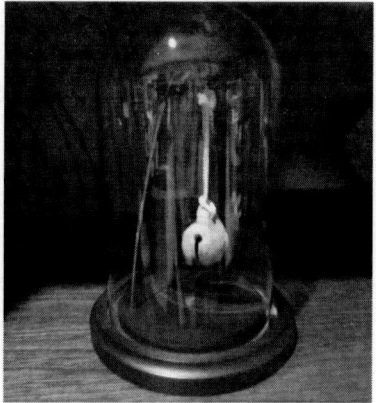

Japanese Bell

over her own hands. Then she offered to dry my hands with her scarf. I chose my own handkerchief. This was a ritual purification before approaching the next god.

Impressed by the size of this ancient idol of 42 feet, I waited for some people to move so I could photograph the Great Buddha alone. Meanwhile, she went to the souvenir stand and returned with a package of postcards. I tried to pay her, but she refused.

Great Buddha

Then smiling and bowing as only the Japanese can, she turned and walked right out of my life as suddenly as she walked in, leaving behind a bewildering but lasting sliver of friendship between two cultures.

ILLUSTRATION

My Expert Opinion

This essay first appeared in The Dallas Morning News *on October 1, 2006.*

It has occurred to me that I have received enough unsolicited mail to overflow a landfill from people who unabashedly tell me they are experts. The scope of these know-it-alls is extraordinary. Some are so chummy that they address me by my first name. Apparently, they know a lot about me, much of which is not so.

The other day, an offer for a video arrived that would teach me "disabling, joint-breaking maneuvers used by Navy Seals." That's supposed to be a tempting skill for a guy who has never even been inclined to kick his wife's cat?

Then, there are the experts who want to show me how to bankrupt Las Vegas at blackjack or grow 8-foot tomato plants on my patio that will produce for six months. Not to be outdone, some segments of the health industry want to reveal their secrets for living to be 120 while staying so sexy that I will be irresistible to beautiful women.

But what really baffles me are the multiple arrivals each week from investment gurus who assure me that I will become wealthy if only I will buy their fool-proof investment system. These proposals always leave me with the persistent question that if these guys really know how to pile it up, why do they need my $69?

These claims got me to thinking about other experts I have encountered over the years. I have noticed that just about any expert eventually gets his comeuppance. In 1933, I watched a government man expertly kill a herd of cattle by hitting each cow between the horns with a ball peen hammer. One cow in her death throes kicked the government man. My family couldn't afford steak, and I wondered why so much beef just went to waste.

The experts said that killing the cows would create a shortage and drive up the price of cattle, which would benefit the cattle raisers, who would have more money to circulate back into the economy. They plowed up cotton for the same reason. I don't know whether this policy helped pull the nation out of the Great Depression. For the answer to that question, you'll have to ask an expert.

I suppose that at times, all of us think we are experts at something. My wife and I set up housekeeping right after she graduated from college. As a home economist student, she had spent six weeks of her last semester experimenting with angel food cake recipes. One day, she asked me to go to the store for a package of cake flour.

I indiscreetly protested, "My mother never had to use any special flour for cakes."

"Yes, and I can bake a better cake than your mother," she sniffed.

Rising to the challenge, I bought the cake flour

for what turned out to be a chocolate cake with chocolate icing. After my wife finished icing it, to her consternation and my considerable amusement, the cake cratered into three large chunks. Later, I committed my second major faux pas as a new husband by gleefully relating the incident to my mother, who severely upbraided me.

Some experts need to be let down gently.

Even I was once an expert, and it turned out to be a humbling experience. My entrance into this elite group began with the delivery of a department store bill, which included a scented advertisement for L'air du Temps perfume. I began to notice its widespread use. I couldn't identify any other fragrances, but I fancied myself an expert at recognizing this one whenever and wherever I encountered it. I even detected it in a restaurant in New Zealand. After the waitress took our order, I said to my wife, "That girl is wearing L'air du Temps." She just shrugged without commenting.

Later, I was telling a friend of mine about this incident as an example of my olfactory prowess. Overhearing the comment, my wife asked, "How come you didn't recognize it when I wore it?"

Surprised, I inquired, "When did you wear it?"

Her testy retort terminated my career as an expert – "I just used up the last of the bottle."

Good Nutrition

This essay first appeared in The Dallas Morning News *on May 19, 2006.*

Of old when folk lay Sick and sorely tried
The doctor gave them physic, and they
died
But here's a happier age: for now we know
Both how to make men sick and keep
them so.

Hilaire Belloc

The prescription plan for senior citizens is the largest social program since the establishment of Medicare. Some people believe neither program has permanent financial sustainability. Furthermore, in the April 2006 issue of *Reader's Digest*, a poll indicated that two-thirds of adults 21 and older said they feel they can't afford to be sick. And hospital emergency rooms are being used for routine office calls by people with no insurance, thereby making it difficult for medical personnel to deal with true emergencies.

One individual can do little to repair the system, but one individual can do much to avoid the system. Here's a case in point:

I was 67 in the summer of 1994 when an annual physical examination at Scott & White Hospital in Temple, Texas, revealed I had prostate cancer. After the shock of the news, I went into complete denial. I thought I had been making healthy choices all of my life—reasonably nutritious food, no alcohol, tobacco or drugs. I still carried the same weight I had in navy boot camp in 1944. From 1989 to 1994, I was a civilian instructor teaching writing to sailors aboard U.S. Navy ships at sea for Central Texas College. The exercise equipment aboard the 13 different ships on which I served occupied much of my spare time. It hadn't been too many months since I had passed a Marine Corps physical readiness test.

How could I possibly have cancer? My urologist told me his lab had found cancer cells in two of the three specimens taken from my prostate. Assuming a mistake had been made, I took the slides to M.D. Anderson Cancer Center in Houston, Texas, for verification. They confirmed the first lab's diagnosis. Still not convinced, I put the slides under a borrowed microscope and compared what I saw with healthy cells and cancerous cells. There had been no mistake.

Urologists at Scott & White, M.D. Anderson, Sloan Kettering and others recommended surgery, radiation or radiated seed implants. The last urologist I consulted wanted to do cryosurgery. Without a consensus, I took matters into my own hands.

My first move was to offer up a simple prayer to God for guidance.

I theorized I had a glitch in my God-given immune system, and fixing the glitch would fix the cancer. Knowing nothing about the Internet at that time, I paid an organization to search the databases of the world for information about prostate cancer. The material I received presented several alternatives to what had been offered me. I decided to follow the nutritional program outlined by a health care professional I hadn't even known existed, the Certified Clinical Nutritionist in Waco, Texas.

I have been cancer-free since shortly after it was detected. Time has proven my case is not unique.

Since a good nutrition program can eliminate cancer from the body, isn't it logical that it could prevent some cancers from developing, thus easing the strain on all insurance programs?

The medical industry is slowly making a paradigm shift for treatment of some ills in the United States. However, people can make their own paradigm shift by taking open-minded responsibility for their own health and investigating all that's available to them.

Shortly before I moved out of the area served by Scott & White in 2004, I got a final checkup from my urologist. As I was about to leave his office, I asked, "Doctor, since most prostate cancer is slow growing, why don't you fellows try nutrition before doing something to compromise a man's immune system?" Smiling, he said, "We're using nutrition now."

.

Lessons from an Absent Father

This essay originally appeared in
The Dallas Morning News *on September 19, 2010.*

Beginning in the 1960s, rising divorce rates and uncommitted relationships between women and men created family wreckage. In the 19th century, Henry Clay Work wrote "Come Home Father," a sad song about a little girl pleading with her father to come home from the bar. Now there seems to be a national plaintive cry, "Father, come home from wherever you are." But some fathers never left their home.

From the time he was born, my son and I developed a bond that continues to this day. When he was 4 years old, I put his first flyable airplane into his hand. A little later I introduced him to U-control aircraft whereby model airplanes flew

Kerry Lee with Stunt Airplane

from two lines sixty feet long extending from his hand to the airplane. We made a good team. I built and repaired them; he flew and crashed them. He became an expert with both stunt and combat models and eventually flew real airplanes.

As a teenager, he often joined me in a mile run after supper. Then we just sat on the front lawn in the dark and talked about issues important to him. This type of camaraderie never existed between my father and me because he walked out of my life when I was 3 years old and my mother was 20. Yet his absence taught me a number of fundamental character traits.

He abandoned us in January 1930 at the beginning of the Great Depression. My mother and I lived on a West Texas farm with her parents. One of my earliest memories is that of sitting at the

J. W. Lee, Father of James V. Lee

end of a row of cotton while my mother picked the cotton. She was a strong woman and could pick about 400 pounds of cotton per day. The going rate was 25 cents a hundred. So at the end of the day she had earned one dollar.

In those hard-scrabble days, even dysfunctional families pulled together and neighbors looked after each other. Consequently, thanks to my absent father, my survival instincts kicked in very early. By age 5, I was pulling my own weight by hoeing cotton, milking cows and doing other farm chores. At age 16, I was fully self-supporting and paying 100 percent of my college expenses. I have never been concerned about staying employed.

Without a father's guidance, I became a keen observer of other people and tried to discern what caused their successes and failures. I became somewhat aloof and a bit judgmental, the extent of which depends on whom you're talking to. But I regard sound judgment a survival skill, and learning to stand on principles and to think for myself have been valuable assets all of my life.

My loyalty to family and friends is at least partially a backlash from the disloyalty of my father who abandoned me. Before I ever started my own family, I had already resolved that I would never walk out on any of them. There are some who contend that friendship is the strongest tie that binds people together. My deceased wife of 60 years was a close friend before we became engaged. I was her full-time caregiver during her lengthy last illness. My two children, as well as numerous friends took notice of that loyalty.

Sometimes people ask me if I have forgiven my father for leaving me at a young age. At first, the question puzzled me somewhat, because I never carried a grudge. He just wasn't present, and nobody ever talked about him. Then someone asked, "Well, did his absence teach you anything." Yes, indeed, my father taught me far more than anybody else can understand. And for that I thank him.

PROCESS

Obesity

This essay first appeared in The Dallas Morning News *on August 2007.*

The Dallas County commissioners have indicated support for replacing Parkland Hospital. Evidently, the hospital has deteriorated considerably since I was a patient there when it was relatively new in 1959. While a new state-of-the-art structure may be most desirable, I hope an equal amount of attention is given to the proficiency of those who will staff the new hospital.

Thanks to my wife's very lengthy illness, I have spent countless hours waiting in hospitals, doctors' offices, labs and rehab facilities watching the personnel at work. All have one thing in common—obesity, a condition responsible for roughly 300,000 deaths per year according to MedicineNet, Inc.

I once spent about three hours in the cafeteria of a local hospital during the lunch period. Out of the dozens of people—including health care workers—who went through the line, only five were not obese. And a series of questions came to mind.

Would I buy a new car from a dealer who drove a jalopy? Would I hire a builder who lived in a shack to construct my dream house? Would I sit through Sunday sermons listening to a known community reprobate?

Since my answer to all those questions is "no," then should I trust my body to the care of people who can't or won't take care of their own bodies? Personally, my answer to that question is also negative.

Fat celebrities have made small fortunes sharing their less than exciting news of their weight loss while countless books, magazine and newspaper articles, and TV ads flood the market with the latest secret for a sexy body. But one would have to be a newcomer to the planet not to know that proper diet and exercise is the universal solution for most people.

But this requires motivation and self discipline, which seemingly is in short supply. Putting aside the threat of death, I don't know why just a bathroom mirror shouldn't be sufficient motivation for anyone.

Apparently, it isn't. Some years ago, I saw a survey by AARP that indicated that elderly overweight people didn't want to lose weight. Rather, they wanted fashionable clothing made in larger sizes. Evidently they got their way. I bought some of the last slim-cut sport shirts from a company that specialized in slim cuts just before they went out of business.

The Dallas area does need a state-of-the-art hospital with Parkland's mission. But along with its brick and mortar, it needs a staff that shows by example the way to healthy living. As the old saying goes, people would rather see a sermon than hear one, including this one.

The Parkland staff doesn't need to wait until various entities pitch in to buy them a new place to work in order to shape up. That can be priority number one right now. By leading the way and setting the bar high, they just might help gin up support for a new facility.

COMPARISON AND CONTRAST

Teenage Angst and Abstinence

This essay first appeared in The Dallas Morning News
on May 11, 2007.

Much has been discussed about the effectiveness of teaching teenagers to abstain from sex before marriage. Proponents are having a hard time
delivering the message because they're preaching
it to the wrong venue—schools. Abstinence before marriage has always been a tenet of God's
law, not man's.

The young people of the 1960s got around His
law by saying God is dead, and if it felt good do it.
Public schools have not decreed that God is dead;
they've simply sent Him packing. Consequently,
to be effective, the message of abstinence must be
delivered elsewhere—homes and churches. It's
not an easy sale.

When I was a teenager at Ackerly High School
at the bottom of the Texas Panhandle, teenagers
understood abstinence to be the norm, and sex
did not fill any part of the school curriculum.
Sex Ed was left up to three churches in that small
farming community, which taught that sex before
marriage was a sin subject to consequences from
God. End of discussion. If anyone violated this
norm of abstinence, no bragging rights came with
it.

Admitedly, we were innocent and ignorant by
present standards, but marriage certificates com-

manded more respect than they do today, and a high percentage of us managed to stay married—in my case sixty years before my wife died. And we just about had STDs whipped until the sexual revolution of the 1960s.

Like everyone else, my own teen years arrived with angst. From the time I was in the seventh grade in 1938 until I entered college in 1943, I lived alone with my mother and step-dad on a farm about two miles west of Ackerly. The intervening years were devoid of much social activity other than church and school. When I was not going to school, there was always farm work to do. About the only thing I knew about girls was what I read in the women's lingerie section of the Montgomery Ward catalogue.

During my sophomore year at Sparenberg, Texas, I was a member of the Future Farmers of America. In the summer of 1941, the entire group took a trip on a flatbed truck to visit Austin, San Antonio, and Corpus Christi. On the way home we stopped for awhile at a little roadside café where a couple was dancing to the music from a jukebox. I heard one of the senior boys say that the girl sure was getting "hot." Later, I was telling my mother about my trip while she was busy in the kitchen. I told her about the "hot" girl in the café. She whirled around with eyes flashing and demanded, "What do you mean?" Taken completely aback, I stammered, "I don't know. That's just what one of the guys said."

Occasionally, in later years, my mother reminded me that I don't have to tell everything I know.

I didn't know my first date in high school was a date. One of my classmates threw a party and said we could invite guests, so I invited a girl from another class. When I arrived at the party, Katy wasn't there, and she never did show up. I didn't think much about it, just figured she'd changed her mind. The next day at school, one of her friends chewed me out and wanted to know why I didn't pick up Katy. Accusingly, she said, "You invited her to the party!"

"Yes," I protested, "but she never showed up. Do you know what happened to her?"

Exasperated, her friend informed me that I was supposed to go by her house and walk her to the party. That didn't make any sense. I lived two miles from school and walked that four-mile round trip every day of the school year through, heat, cold, sand storm, or whatever. Katy lived only two blocks from the party. She was a healthy girl, and I didn't know why she needed my help to get there.

After that, Katy seemed somewhat distant.

I had only two double dates in high school, and both turned out to be more embarrassing than enlightening. Following graduation, I enrolled in Texas Tech. in Lubbock, Texas, and joined a fairly large Sunday school class. Since I was carrying a full academic load and working at two jobs to pay for my college expenses, I had little time for social life. But I finally found the time and courage to ask a cute girl from my class to go to the movie.

I was almost seventeen and a man of the world. I knew enough to go by the girl's house and walk her to the picture show. Afterward, we walked back to her house. It was one of those nights in Lubbock when the air was cool, crisp, and still. A full moon filled the cloudless sky, a perfect night to be in the presence of a beautiful young girl. When we got to her house, she turned her back to the door and just stood there with her face tilted up to me. I simply said good night and left.

My social skills were slow in developing.

But I had a couple of good reasons for not kissing that girl. In the first place, I didn't know how. Secondly, I figured she would tell one or more of her friends. Then everybody in my Sunday school class would find out about it, and my Christian reputation would be ruined.

None of this is to suggest that today's teens should wallow in sexual ignorance, but those who do abstain from sex until marriage and stay married won't have a past marred by regrets, STDs—or a disappointed God.

Joy Versus Fun

Iago, the villain in Shakespeare's play *Othello*, speaks the following words:

> *"Who steals my purse steals trash; 'tis*
> *something, nothing;*
> *'Twas mine, 'tis his, and has been slave to*
> *thousands;*
> *But he that filches from me my good name*
> *Robs me of that which not enriches him,*
> *And makes me poor indeed."*

Although steal, filch, and rob have the same general meaning, each has its own nuance, a distinction that sets the words apart from each other. Shakespeare was a master at choosing just the right word to convey exact meanings.

People in general are not so precise. For example, the words joy and fun fall into the general category of a sense of well being. Yet close examination shows them to be quite different from each other:

> *Joy is a spiritual quality defined by*
> *universal singularity.*
> *Fun is a humanistic quality defined by*
> *individual singularity.*

Joy is that quality of life that connects the human spirit with the Spirit of God. Consequently, it applies to all people of all ages at all locations. Here's an example: As recorded in the Book of Acts of the Apostles in the Bible, Paul and Silas exemplified joy by singing after they had been beaten with rods and chained in a prison cell in the city of Philippi. The incongruity of expressing joy in the face of such adversity favorably impressed the other prisoners as well as their jailor. Thus joy has the power to transcend whomever it touches, even those under great duress. Its moral compass rests firmly in the concept of Deity.

But joy does not require enduring hardship. It manifests itself in countless ways that are not always appreciated because our focus may be elsewhere. Nature provides unceasing moments of joy if we but take them: a rainbow after a refreshing shower, the sunrise or sunset, the constant reconfiguration of clouds, songs of birds, fireflies at twilight, a full moon over an ocean of whitecaps, horses running free, or the granite spires of a canyon. The interaction of people also offers endless moments of joy such as the giddy laughter of a little child, the look of love on the face of a new bride, an elderly couple holding hands in church, or an attentive ear for someone who may be hurting.

Fun, on the other hand, knows no such universality. Its meaning varies from person to person. Fun for a teenager might be a ride on a roller coaster, while fun for a psychopath might be murder. Without a generally accepted moral compass, fun can be whatever the participant wants it to be.

We live in a culture obsessed by entertainment, but so have other cultures through the ages. The problem with fun is that it can take that which is essentially harmless to all concerned and turn it into something sordid and diabolical. The Roman Empire with its gladiatorial contests corrupted an entire civilization in the name of entertainment. Ignoring the lessons of history, the human junk pile in America is stacked with derelicts who gave their lives in the elusive search of pleasure.

William Congreve, stated in The Mourning Bride in 1697 that, "Music has charms to soothe a savage breast," And what heart is so dull that it has not been stirred by beautiful music? Yet who can deny that some of what passes for modern music can only degrade the heart that it touches? The glorification in song of that which obviously destroys society sends countless numbers of people to their graves with beautiful music still in them. They never learned to sing for joy because they searched in the wrong places. Andrew Fletcher an 18th Century Scottish Parliamentarian patriot expressed the power of music with these words: "Let me write the songs of a nation, and I care not who writes its laws." Thus music that expresses joy has the power to elevate an entire nation.

Fun has its fleeting moments of satisfaction but may be contrary to human law, while joy, against which there is no law, endures now and forever.

Making Prison Look Easy

This essay first appeared in The Dallas Morning News *on December 22, 2006.*

Choosing punishment to fit the crime has been an age-old challenge. Recent times have produced very different examples of punishment for the same crime. A few years ago, an international debate arose when the authorities in Singapore severely canned a young American for defacing public property with graffiti. Apparently no American has repeated this crime, so the punishment must have been effective.

When four young men from Wylie, Texas, ages 18 to 20, senselessly defaced property with graffiti, they were charged with a felony that, if convicted, will have serious consequences for their U.S. citizenship. The 20-year-old man stated in *The Dallas Morning News*, "That seems kind of harsh for just some kids."

If a person can vote and wear a combat uniform at age 18, when does a kid become a man? A very high percentage of "just kids" in the U.S. military carry the burden of defending the very society that the four young men chose to desecrate. I wonder if they might prefer Singapore-style justice.

Being aware of cruel and unusual punishment performed throughout the world, the framers of our Constitution prohibited such beatings. Although a felony conviction may also seem cruel and unusual to the person who receives it, such punishment becomes insignificant when compared to beatings, which had been practiced for centuries at the time our nation was founded.

I have seen some of these torture devices. A Tokyo museum situated inside a replica of the Eiffel Tower contains an unusually sadistic torture contrivance from an ancient age that would repulse the sensitivities of any normal person. Tormenters placed a victim on his back under a giant spike-studded wheel. As the wheel turned, it slowly shredded the victim.

The castle at Peniscola (pronounced Payny-eescola), Spain, sits on a peninsula overlooking a small harbor. Residences and shops line the narrow cobblestone street rutted by wagon wheels that wind up to the castle. The castle-top affords a commanding view of the sandy beach washed by clear, aquamarine water, so it's easy to see why the castle was built there. Most of the rooms were devoid of furniture, but the room that made the greatest impact on me was the dungeon. As I gazed through the iron grate to the room below, I understood for the first time the horror of being left to rot in solitary, indefinite confinement in a stone box.

Warwick Castle in England now serves as a museum. But from the beginning of its construction in 1066, it played key roles in the various English wars fought over several centuries. On display in Warwick is a device formerly used throughout Europe that caused even the most hardened criminals to break down. Immobilized in a suit of iron straps, the victim was hung outdoors without water or food and subjected to heat, cold, rain, insects, birds or passer-by tormentors until he died.

Although the United States has legislated against cruel and unusual punishment and has set a low bar for its definition, the practice still prevails elsewhere. Leon Uris, in his book *The Haj*, describes punishment still practiced in the Middle East that's too gruesome to relate in this essay.

No one likes to be punished for anything, no matter the justification, but Americans can be grateful to live in a society that attempts to be reasonable and fair. The world is intolerant of anarchy. That's why natural and manmade laws exist. If people of any age fail to discipline themselves, somebody or some event eventually will do it for them. The kindest discipline is self-discipline.

Reflected Wisdom

ANALOGY

Origins for Sensitivity

I have seen the arctic where impenetrable fog
Blends with turgid clouds to overlay snow-blanketed
   mountains,
Devoid of all movement by man, bird, or beast,
Where biting, blinding chill reigns over awesome beauty in
   serene silence.

I have felt hearts so cold that no warmth can pen-
   etrate,
Where no acts of humanity can fill the void,
Where no words of love or entreaty stir the soul,
Where no beauty abounds to compensate for icy iso-
   lation.

I have seen the blazing sun in a cloudless sky,
On an ocean devoid of all movement,
Where the air is so thin that birds cannot fly,
And unbearable heat reigns over supreme silence.

I have felt hot hatred that seared a heart
That deigned to cool the torrent of passion
Where a chasm of vanity forever claimed
A friendship that might have been.

I have been entranced by a full moon
Resplendent through scudding clouds
Where the vigor of a cool breeze
Foamed the waves of a pelagic sea.

I have known the comfort of divine love,
Which bathed in its splendor the human heart
To unlock the treasury of compassion
To satisfy my innate yearning to serve my Creator.

DIVISION AND CLASSIFICATION

Who's a Texan?

A new arrival to Texas admitted that he likes the people but thinks Texas drivers display a lot of bad habits on the roads. I got to wondering which Texans he was talking about: those who were born here, those who moved here from somewhere else, or temporary residents. Anyone not born in Texas—and they number in the millions—brought their driving habits with them. So to blame poor driving on Texans in general is a broad, illogical indictment.

People born in Texas have always been a special breed, believing that Texas isn't just a state. It's a state of mind. We have deep roots in Texas. We are descendants of those early settlers, such as Stephen F. Austin's colony of 300 households from the United States. Some of our forebears were cowboys, gamblers, thieves, fortune hunters, fugitives from justice, and other colorful professions.

We believe any legend that portrays Texas in a complimentary manner. Col. William B. Travis, commander of the garrison at the Alamo in 1836, really did draw that line in the sand. And every man in the garrison stepped over that line to defend the Alamo.

We believe that the Texas Rangers are the best lawmen in the world. Who else has the reputation of "One mob, one Ranger?"

We believe that God created Texas first out of

the good stuff and everybody else got the left-overs. That's why there's a sign in Hondo, Texas, that reads, "This is God's country. Don't drive through it like hell."

Newcomers show up with bumper stickers that read, "I wasn't born in Texas, but I got here as fast as I could." That's not true. They waited until the state was generally air conditioned. How else could Yankees have made their fortunes in Houston?

Some of these newcomers from other states have a bit of trouble assembling into Texas culture. At parents' night at school, one mother was heard to ask the teacher, "Students don't have to take a course in the history of the state we moved from. Why does my child have to take a course in Texas history?" The teacher gave her the only logical answer, "Because it's worth knowing, ma'am." Another reason for knowing Texas history is to prevent visitors from asking, "Why did they build the Alamo downtown?"

Temporary residents in Texas come here for several reasons. The Snowbirds from up north greatly expand the population in the Rio Grande Valley each year to escape the North, which is uninhabitable during the winter months. They live in their travel trailers and become a unique part-year community.

But people south of Texas come here neither to congregate as a small society nor to seek acceptance into Texan culture. Basically, some are just long distance commuters funneling billions of dollars into the Mexican economy. Shipping their low income people to the United States is Mexico's way of redressing their loss of a lot of their territory in the war with the United States in 1848. Old grudges sometimes die hard.

Another group of residents temporarily invade Texas because they know that Texans are the most hospitable people on earth exemplified by our state motto: "Friendship." The Texas legislature adopted that motto in 1930. I guess by then most of the "colorful" characters had passed on to their reward—some being abetted by "Old Sparky," the obsolete electric chair in Huntsville.

Visitors find much to see and do in Texas, including all the once-thriving small towns clinging to life with their historic districts. Some towns do this very effectively. A woman can walk down Main Street in Salado, a former college town, and find anything she doesn't need for her home. People come from everywhere to fill up their SUVs with the stuff. And while the women shop, their husbands test their skills on the town's superb golf course. Then at night, they can dine in nationally acclaimed restaurants.

The drawing power of Texas is such that some segments of every ethnic group in the world reside here. Whether people come to Texas to make a life, to make a buck, or just to have fun, oppor-

tunities flourish to satisfy whatever they're looking for. And if you don't like the way some people
drive—well, just stay out of their way.

DEFINITION

Kid Fun

This essay first appeared in The Dallas Morning News *on February 2, 2007.*

A friend sent me an e-mail saying that two days after Christmas her children were driving her crazy because they were so bored. She wanted them back in school ASAP!

Kids today have too many doodads that stifle the kind of creativity that prevents boredom. I'm not suggesting a return to those thrilling days of yesteryear, but it seems to me that some of the things my generation did might trigger a few ideas for today's youngsters.

When I was a little kid, toys were something owned by rich kids who wouldn't share. So some of us improvised toys with our imagination. For example, I owned a fantasy "pedaling car" that took my 5-year-old mind to some faraway places. It was OK for normal cruising, but if I wanted to go somewhere in a hurry, I just put an engine in it. To an adult onlooker, it was just an old brown snuff bottle.

Every farm in West Texas had a scrap pile that was useful for supplying just the right piece of wood, metal or wire to

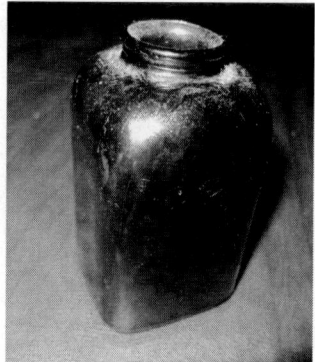

Snuff Bottle

fix something. When we boys went home from church with one another on Sundays, we explored the host's scrap pile and compared it with our own. Somebody else's scrap pile always contained unique items that could hold our interest for a few hours. And sometimes we even found something useful for our juvenile needs.

In those days, all the farms had milk cows. Their calves were always in the pen during the day while the cows were in the pasture. At night, they were reversed. Often, on one of those warm Sunday afternoons, somebody decided it was rodeo time. Riding calves without any kind of rodeo tack proved challenging, so we didn't stay on board very long. Cow patty evidence on our clothes certified that fact to disapproving adults who reprimanded us—both for harassing the calves and soiling our clothes.

After I moved to Lubbock with my grandparents, I discovered roller skates—the adjustable kind with steel wheels on ball bearings that were clipped to our shoe soles. Skates always ranked high on the Santa Claus wish list. Kids with skates weren't bored, and almost none were fat. In those days, any town worth its name had sidewalks everywhere. So kids had ready-made places to skate. When one of the skates inevitably broke, we took the remaining skate apart and attached two wheels to each end of a board. Then we nailed an upright stick to the board and called it a scooter. This must have been the beginning of modern skateboards that now enjoy widespread prohibited use.

A vacant lot in the neighborhood provided us with a place for sandlot softball. Since we never had enough players for two teams, we played scrub. No adults ever showed up to spoil the fun.

After softball season, we took up shinny, a game much like hockey, except the puck was a tin can, and the hockey stick was whatever kind of stick we could locate. Our shins took a beating. I guess that's why we called it shinny.

Then there were the fights—rubber gun fights. In those days all tires had inner tubes made of real rubber. We cut up old tubes into wide bands and affixed them to our crude, handmade wooden pistols. No matter how much we stretched the bands, they wouldn't fly very far. So nobody ever got hurt.

Learning that fun is what you make it is a prelude to learning that life is what you make it. People who grow up understanding that sometimes discover that they are able to make their own breaks.

CAUSE AND EFFECT

Real Men

Occasionally, I meet a young woman who asks, "Where are all the real men?" There used to be a pathway for developing boys into men. When I was a teenage member of the Future Farmers of America, the membership was all male. After I entered the business world, I joined the Junior Chamber of Commerce (Jaycees), which was an all male organization. As a business owner, I eventually joined the Rotary Club, which was all male. The male camaraderie of these, and organizations like them, had a major impact on maturing boys into men. But women now make up part of the membership of all of these organizations, and the male camaraderie, if it exists at all, has been diluted. Rotary International protested the inclusion of women in its membership all the way to the U. S. Supreme Court and lost. I'm not aware that men have insisted on joining any traditional women's organizations.

Since the so-called women's movement started the 1960s, millions of women have thrust themselves into roles traditionally occupied by men. It's a world where women, in demanding equal rights, have become universal competitors of men—a legal and moral outcome. But the plaintive question of young women indicates an unintended consequence. We now have girly men and Tom boy women.

So the young woman searching for what she considers a real man often finds her choices limited to someone looking for a sex object with no commitments or someone who has already allowed himself to be emasculated by a woman. When a man refuses to take the lead in a courtship or marriage relationship, the woman will always emasculate him. She can't help it. It's her self-preservation instinct.

Another factor that plays havoc with manhood is the rise in single moms who inadvertently emasculate their sons before they move out into the world. Without a male role model in their homes, these "mamas' boys" often rush back home to mommy at the first sign of trouble in their marriages.

A mother should never allow her son in her house under those circumstances. It's quite possible that a man's wife further emasculated him after their marriage. She could have done this by trying to compete with him and putting him down instead of supporting him.

The proposed solution that follows has its roots in Christian theology, which may polarize those who accept Christianity from those who don't.

The husband must assert his manhood and take the lead, but for him to have any expectation that his wife will follow his lead, he must "...love his wife just as Christ loved the church and gave himself for it." (Eph 5:25) A woman married to such a man has no reason to be in competition with him. A man so devoted to his wife that he would unhesitatingly die for her can expect her loving support and encouragement for meeting the objectives of the family. However, in order for a man to merit that support, it's vital that he be considerate of the concerns of his wife so that they arrive at a mutually agreeable means of attaining that objective. The roles played in such a relationship will bring out the best in both parties: strong and noble traits in the husband; caring and nurturing traits in the wife.

When a man takes the lead and the woman follows in loving support, he will go out into the world to get whatever she wants and just give it to her. That's how men are wired.

A woman who understands Godly submission to her husband can take an ordinary man and turn him into a genius. Here's an example. Nancy Davis had a promising career as an actress when she married Ronald Reagan. She gave it up to be a loving, submissive helpmate to Ronald. And what did she get out of the deal? Just First Lady to the most powerful man in the world while being consistently voted the most admired woman in the world! Although she made significant accomplishments apart from the presidency, it was obvious that she absolutely adored her husband. And it's questionable whether Ronald Reagan would ever have become governor of California or president of the United States without Nancy at his side.

Men need to look for opportunities to be together as men supporting each other's manhood. Smart women will encourage such activity and improve their own prospects of finding the real men they're looking for.

ARGUMENTATION

The Road Not Taken

This essay first appeared in The Dallas Morning News *on August 10, 2007.*

"Two roads diverged in a wood, and I—I took the one less traveled by, and that has made all the difference."

Robert Frost

News sources give Americans their "crisis fix" almost daily with the basic message: "Things ain't right. Somebody oughta do something." In one of its many forecasts, the federal government predicts a shortage of 24,000 doctors and about one million nurses by 2020. Broad scale changes in the health care industry are necessary to avoid this crisis. Otherwise you may become a "victim."

If people provided as much preventive maintenance for their bodies as they do their automobiles, they wouldn't need so many doctors and nurses.

Have you ever noticed the difference between the health ads on TV for people vs. animals? The people ads show folks in some state of misery and offer a pill that comes with all kinds of unwanted side effects. The drug will not cure, but the pharmaceutical company promises to make you more comfortable.

Conversely, the animal ads show happy dogs

and cats eagerly gobbling up food that's guaranteed to contain all the necessary vitamins and minerals to maintain a healthy pet. Since the animals eat nutritious food and usually get plenty of exercise, they enjoy virility into old age and seldom get sick.

CEOs of pharmaceutical companies ought to be thankful for junk food, all-you-can-eat restaurants and lazy people for delivering the highest percentage profit margins of all corporate groups in America. Their tenure literally depends on the reaction by Wall Street analysts to the corporations' quarterly results. So the sicker the people, the greater the sales and profits, and the more secure the jobs of the CEOs.

According to a July 23, 2007 article in *The Dallas Morning News*, drug companies sheltered billions of their profits in overseas tax havens, which are out of the reach of the IRS. For many Americans who are responsible for these profits, drug costs have already reached a crisis level. The success of drug companies is vested in attempting to fix the body after it's broken.

But therein lies the challenge. Some doctors I have spoken with over the years make no claim to healing people. Rather, they try to create conditions whereby the body heals itself. They tell me that certain drugs may arrest a disease, but without the building blocks from good nutrition and the flushing of poisons through exercise, the body has limited ability to heal itself, and thus a continual need exists to increase the drugs to deal with a deteriorating outcome. So the key is a lifestyle that avoids—to the greatest extent possible—the use of expensive drugs, doctors, or nurses.

Being as healthy as a dog or cat isn't all that tough. Nutritionists recommend that we eat five helpings of fruits and vegetables daily. How about picking five from a list such as this: apple, orange, grapes, berries, banana, carrot, tomato, celery, broccoli, cauliflower. You don't even have to fire up the stovetop. And all of it fits into a brown bag.

As for exercise, "Just do it." "It" can take many forms. For years, I made frequent trips by car throughout the United States and developed an exercise routine that could be performed in any Motel 6. A good regimen could include Tai Chi and/or calisthenics seven days a week, plus weight training three times a week interspersed with walking/jogging. All can be accomplished in and around the home. The full routine takes a little less than an hour—about the same amount of time you spent in P.E. in school.

The key is to find the self-discipline to do what you already know how to do to stay healthy.

Life Ain't Fair

When I was a high school teacher, I caught one of my straight "A" students sharing information with two of her friends on a test. I gave all three girls a zero. Her father, an M.D., called me saying I was being too severe with his daughter. After patiently listening to his objection, I ended the conversation with these words. "Sir, I should think you'd be more concerned about your daughter's integrity than a mark on a piece of paper that nobody is going to remember three months from now."

By contrast a Chinese doctor demonstrated the high esteem Chinese people hold for teachers by calling me to apologize for his eighth-grade daughter who failed a test. He said he had spanked the child. I said, "Doctor, perhaps you should have come to the school house and spanked the teacher. Most of the class did poorly on that test, which tells me one of two things went wrong. Either it was a poor test or else I did not give adequate preparation for it. Your child is an excellent student. Don't worry about her grade. We'll review the material."

When I was in graduate school, one of my professors had to leave the room for an extended period for some kind of emergency during the final exam. Nobody in the room made a move to cheat. Since then, I have witnessed a downward spiral in American morals accelerated by the 1960s when young people declared that God is dead. Since God is no longer welcome in schools, where is the foundation for student morality? Certainly not in the quicksand of situation ethics. Many of that generation of Americans also declared that "character doesn't matter." Some now occupy the highest levels of American government, private businesses, and education. Because of their disparagement of character, corruption in all of these organizations has become the greatest peril facing the United States. People of good character are the ones who are best equipped to deal with problems within the country or foes outside the country.

Cheating in school ultimately plays out in the professions as well as other vocations. For many years, I was the full-time caretaker of my chronically ill wife, now deceased. Although a very high level of integrity does exist in the medical community, I've seen doctors and labs hijack Medicare and insurance companies simply because they could get away with it, and I wonder how they conducted themselves as students.

Here are a couple of examples. Three pain specialists over a period of years put my wife through physical, expensive misery before I accidentally discovered her musculoskeletal pain could be alleviated by 4000 IU daily of inexpensive Vitamin D. A report saying as much was published years earlier by the Mayo Clinic. Either the pain specialists knew about the report or they didn't. Ignorance or greed—take your pick. Another doctor nearly killed my wife, and would have, except for an alert nurse. The medical profession has no monopoly on such incompetence. Villains exist in all businesses and professions.

Students with no spiritual roots will do whatever it takes to graduate from prestigious universities. Some of them line their office walls with framed, impressive looking diplomas. If all I have to go on are the certificates that grace these offices, the only thing I know for sure is that those who have them were clever enough to get through the system. So, the message to the public is *caveat emptor*. The message to the honest student is that life ain't fair—never has been and never will be. More importantly, he needs to understand that cheaters become intellectual cripples who are incapable of self-respect or honest service to his fellow citizens. Armed with that understanding a young man or woman can learn to make sound judgments about people and what they profess to be—and deal with them accordingly.

.

What's the Difference?

This essay first appeared in The Dallas Morning News *on December 15, 2006.*

An acquaintance told me that she became a schoolteacher because she "wanted to make a difference." Countless teachers, politicians, social workers, doctors, preachers and journalists—to name a few—have chosen their life's work for the same reason. It seems that merely tossing out the statement is supposed to induct one into the realm of the noblesse.

But this unadorned avowal always leaves me wondering what this person's agenda is. Will the teacher passionately guide the students in the discovery of truth, or will she present her own version of truth? Can the conservative politician make a difference diametrically opposed to that of a liberal politician? Is the journalist going to make a difference by fearlessly reporting factual news, or will he color the facts with his own bias?

This stand-alone idea is meaningless. Rather, its meaning is derived from the action, if any, that follows. Adolph Hitler, Joseph Stalin, Benito Mussolini and other infamous heads of states were allowed by their own countrymen to make differences that devastated the whole world. And the rationale that brought these people to power hasn't vanished with the vanquished.

Two generations ago, John Dillinger imposed

his own idea of making a difference by becoming America's Public Enemy No. 1. Other gangsters, such as Al Capone, made similar differences.

Starry-eyed idealists who really want to be taken seriously need to embellish their stated objectives with a clearly defined goal with at least the broad steps for achieving it. But I suspect that many have not set a goal. They have merely set a wish.

Likewise, declarations to make any part of the world "better" have a hollow ring.

I learned this truism as a sophomore vocational agriculture student in high school. Mr. Owens, my ag teacher, prohibited the use of the word "better" when judging livestock. Students had to give specific reasons why the anatomy of one cow was superior to that of another.

And so it is with ideas. The difference between a high-sounding platitude and a clearly defined political goal and the means for achieving it is the difference between a political hack and a political leader. Enduring ideas rise above the level of mere propaganda. And ideas that enrich society avoid appealing to the lowest level of public knowledge. Rather, the proponents of such ideas should recognize the responsibility to know the truth of their subject in order to enlighten those who are less informed. Otherwise, the advocate risks the danger of falling into one of two groups: ignorance or hypocrisy.

People who say they want to make a difference

often harbor an unspoken "what's in it for me?" motive. Although history abounds with examples of people who have spent their entire lives in purely altruistic endeavors, they seem to be a miniscule minority. For example, does anyone really believe that a person seeking congressional office is motivated solely by the desire to make a difference or "to give something back?" If he didn't steal it, there's nothing to give back, because whatever he has was obtained in a fair exchange of time, talent and service. So doesn't the answer reside in the massive amount of money required to win the office and the fact that once in office, the congressman immediately begins campaigning for re-election?

And is there really any need to elaborate on multi-millionaire preachers who extract small sums from widows? Or some social workers who teach self-supporting, low-income people how to get on welfare in order to secure their own jobs?

The desire to make a difference in improving the lot of any segment of humanity actually can be a noble idea. Motives don't have to be relegated to Utopia. They need only to be examined honestly before launching into some cause. Service above self is an old idea worth repeating because people who occupy an honorable place in history are remembered for something constructive they did for somebody else. And that's a difference worth recognizing.

Deaf

This essay first appeared in The Dallas Morning News *on July 13, 2007.*

A high school principal once told me that a teachers' meeting was good place to die because you wouldn't miss anything. Lately, I've noticed that my once-perfect ability to hear is causing me to miss some of the things said in group meetings that I would like to hear. So I had my hearing tested by an otolaryngologist. That's a fancy name for and ear, nose, and throat doctor (ENT). Learning how to pronounce the word may improve my social status. He told me that I had only partial ability to hear some tones in the higher range, such as women's voices. Although that wasn't good news, I know a few husbands who would consider it an asset. The good news was that he didn't think I needed to hang a $7,000 device in my ear.

Over the years, my wife has accused me of not remembering some things she has told me. I'm not about to admit to senility. Probably, my thoughts at the time were more entertaining than what she was saying, and I voluntarily tuned her out. But I'm not going to admit that to her either.

Some parents have offspring that they think are sometimes deaf, but that credits the kids with more power than they deserve. They're just alone in their thoughts. I think there are times when everybody prefers to be alone in their thoughts.

A while back I walked into a café for breakfast. The conversation with the waitress went like this.

"May I take your order?"

"Yes. I'd like two scrambled eggs with toast and cup of hot tea."

"How'd you want the eggs?"

"Scrambled."

"Biscuits or toast?"

"Toast."

"You want cream with your coffee?"

"Hot tea, please."

Another time I filled my grocery store shopping cart with everything I needed, except for one item that I intended to ask about when I checked out. Before the clerk began to scan my items, she asked the customary, "Did you find everything you wanted?" I replied, "No." She just started scanning without making a response. I let it go.

These two events suggest that most of us are on automatic pilot in repetitive, mundane situations, requiring little thought. We're so used to the routine, such as driving in traffic that an unexpected jolt catches us off guard and makes us look foolish. Like the time as a college student I stopped my motorcycle at a Y in the street of an unfamiliar town to allow what I thought was a funeral procession to pass. However, the line of cars taking the right fork was only a part of the evening rush. As I swung back around to proceed, suddenly a car took the left fork. The crash bars on my big 1947 Indian wrinkled the car's front fender, creased the left door, and dented the rear quarter panel. Both my motorcycle and I were unharmed. Two cops witnessed the accident. They agreed to forget what they saw if I would pay for damages to the car. I settled with other driver and parted much more alert.

Most world travelers can relate incidences of miscommunication between languages. Sometimes they're embarrassing or even deadly but often are funny. An acquaintance of mine who speaks fluent Japanese took one of his naval buddies to a Japanese disco. His friend admired a pretty girl there and wanted to give her his phone number, so my acquaintance told him what to say. Since the music was very loud, his friend had to repeat himself several times. Finally, he was virtually shouting when the music suddenly stopped and he garbled the words he was supposed to say. To the great amusement of a packed house, he had just told the girl, "I am a toilet." They've been married for a number of years.

Expressing ourselves gives our egos a needed stroke, but only if our words fall on an attentive listener. One of the most sincere compliments we can give each other is simply to listen without interruption to what the other person is saying.

Kindness to Strangers

This essay first appeared in The Dallas Morning News *on October 5, 2007.*

Young people often overlook one of their most important advantages: the goodwill of adults they don't even know. We are people who are silently evaluating the words and behavior of people who are worthy of our time, talent, influence and resources. There are many of us altruistic-minded people who are a bit like an alert bird dog just waiting for an opportunity. We show up in the most unexpected places. Here's a simple example:

I stopped for a cup of coffee at a quick stop right after school was out for the summer. A fresh-faced 16-year-old boy served me with the enthusiasm of one delivering pheasant under glass to a king. I called him aside, complimented his behavior, and gave him a $20 tip. Astonished, he said, "I can't accept that!"

"Sure you can," I replied. He looked questioningly at his boss who nodded her agreement. One of the other customers asked incredulously, "Was he really that good?" I responded, "Yes, he was, and if he treats everybody with the same attitude he displayed toward me, he has a very bright future in whatever field he chooses."

Although the $20 meant little to me, consider the possible ripples from that simple gesture. The boy most likely told all of his friends, some of whom may derive inspiration from him. His boss probably held him up as a positive example to other employees, some of whom may realize that service to customers is more important to their future than entertaining themselves on company time by conversing in a foreign language. And you can be sure that his mother spread the word that she had raised an outstanding son. Furthermore, isn't it probable that the boy will take this incident into adulthood and pass it on in ways we can't even envision?

You never know who is watching you for an opportunity to be of some help. I recall with embarrassment when, as a college student, I jokingly made a comment to a man who could have influenced a potential career. Taking the comment seriously, he considered me a fool and terminated the relationship. That must have been the origin of my realization of the power possessed by adult strangers to boost the development of young people.

Here's an example of another young man who blew it. We were engaged in a conversation about computers in a retail outlet. I mentioned that my computer had a glitch that had baffled a couple of people who had looked at it. He was sure he could help. He accepted my offer of payment for his time. He never showed up for the appointment, nor did he ever call to say why. I learned from a third party that he chose to do something else.

It won't matter much how many years this

young man goes to school or how many letters he has after his name if he makes a habit of treating other people as irrelevant or unimportant. It appears he is already handicapping his future because he has failed to learn a fundamental principle of successful living: Make promises sparingly, and faithfully perform those you do make—no matter how trivial.

Other positive examples have blessed my life over the years—some small, some quite significant, ranging from financial relief to career enhancement. Most are known only to me, and some of those have faded from memory. Not all have had a happy ending.

I once encountered a young woman who had a vexing problem that I could have fixed right on the spot, but she wouldn't stop whining long enough for me to get a word in edgewise. Finally, I walked away, and she never knew what she missed.

Good Samaritans don't wear nametags.

Young people need to learn early in life to conduct themselves with a measure of wisdom. There is a time to be cool for your mutual benefit with peers, but there is also a time to just cool it, and think not about the person you are, but about the person you want to become.

You may never encounter me or anyone like me, but how do you know you won't? If you do, what kind of impression are you going to make?

Reflected Wisdom

120

Tough Love

This essay first appeared in The Dallas Morning News *on June 15, 2007.*

Ben Shott of *The New York Times* released the results of the annual General Social Survey on February 25, 2007, which showed in part that about 71% of people in the United States approve of spanking their children. Although this method of discipline has received high approval ratings all the way back to King Solomon, about 29% of people in our permissive society condemn spanking for any cause.

I suspect that those who are antipathetic to spanking relate it to child abuse. Having been on the receiving end of beatings from enraged relatives, I understand and oppose such treatment.

But all of us have witnessed parents in the mall who seemingly were oblivious to their screaming child who had been denied some trinket. Those of us who grew up with corporeal punishment being the norm know that about two firm swats to the backside of the screamer usually results in sniffling silence. I sometimes wonder if parents ignore such children with the expectation that they will eventually understand the futility of throwing a fit or whether they are intimidated by the 29% who oppose spanking and who might alert Child Protective Services if they saw a kid being swatted.

I have heard of a few cases of people who have never spanked anybody. Assuming all those children grew up to be law abiding adults, I congratulate them with a fervent wish that such were the universal norm. Effective discipline requires setting the rules or conditions that include some kind of firm enforcement by clearly understood consequences, which may or may not include spanking. Both of my grown children received spankings from both parents when they were children. When I asked my daughter if they did any good, she replied, "Well, I think some of it was good, but I recall some whippings that I think were clearly over the top. But that's the way it goes. Parents aren't perfect." Obviously, she knows how to dispense parental remorse.

Of course, spanking is not the only way of expressing tough love and it only works up to a certain age anyway. Methods of tough love are limited only by the imagination of adults in authority.

While I was teaching in high school, a star basketball player failing my economics course came to me with tears in his eyes begging me to adjust his grade so he could play in the upcoming game. I kindly but firmly responded, "Don't ever put yourself at the mercy of a school teacher, or for that matter, don't ever put yourself at the mercy of any other human being. You do what's expected of you, what's required of you, and then you can command whatever privileges to which you're entitled." Sitting out the game didn't hurt him and may have taught him a valuable lesson.

Discipline delayed can result in discipline distress. During my years of teaching aboard navy ships, I met a young sailor who credited the navy with keeping him out of trouble. As a 15-year-old ruffian of immature judgment, he thought he was tough enough to take on his dad, a U. S. Navy Seal. After the short fight ended in full view of cheering neighbors, my young friend required hospitalizing and wore one arm in a sling for a while. His contribution to the fight was to vomit on his father. While his mother and younger brother took him to the hospital, his dad went out for a beer. They've had a good father/son relationship ever since.

Children who start out rebellious to parental authority don't always need the trauma of mortal combat to shape up. Sometimes a wayward offspring, like the biblical prodigal son, just has to hit bottom in some figurative pig sty before coming to his senses. Upon returning home, he needs the welcoming arms of a father and mother who never gave up on him.

Even though parents may accept the admonition to "train up a child in the way he should go, and when he is old, he will not depart from it" (Prov. 22:6), they don't always succeed, either with or without spankings. Because parental love may obscure the defects in character that are clearly evident to society at large, often, whenever a criminal's behavior finally catches up with him, somewhere there are parents second guessing themselves, "Were we too permissive, or were we too strict, and did we apply any of it with love?"

If life had only a rewind button.

Just Say No

This essay first appeared in The Dallas Morning News
on April 5, 2007.

When heroin use among students of Plano ISD in the late 1990s made national news, Dr. Larry Alexander, a Plano, Texas, ER doctor at that time, made hard-hitting oral and film presentations to area students explaining and showing in graphic detail the results of heroin use. The presentation ended with a student who had died from using heroin being zipped up in a body bag. It shocked the PISD students who responded by curtailing heroin use.

The Dallas Morning News has reported on a dangerous new substance called "cheese" that threatens the current generation of Dallas-area students, thus proving the necessity of ceaseless vigilance to protect our young people. The new menace may be even more dangerous than heroin because it's so cheap that anyone can buy it.

When Nancy Reagan graced the White House as First Lady, she received considerable ridicule from critics who characterized the idea of just saying "no" to drugs as naive. Just saying "no" is not a substitute for knowledge, whether from parents or school personnel, but the word "no" when coupled with knowledge is a powerful weapon.

I learned its effectiveness during the years I was a salesman. Salesmen are trained to say "why" when a prospect says "no" and will keep asking "why" as long as a prospect continues to say "no" and follows with a reason. Citing a reason out of politeness exposes one's vulnerability.

If you really don't want to buy drugs or any other product or service, or engage in any kind of activity that compromises your health or reputation, the key is simply to say "no" and shut up. When the inevitable "why" is spoken, the proper response is something like, "It doesn't matter," or "it's not your concern," or "you don't need to know" or simply a silent disapproving look. But under no circumstance give a reason, because no salesman in the world, including a drug dealer, can rebut an unembellished "no."

If the pressure is coming from a peer group, saying "no" and walking away is especially effective. If you lose the group, you haven't lost anything. They weren't your friends.

Consider the type of person who tempts others to use drugs. Drug dealers, including your "friends" who want you to party with them, know that drugs can destroy everything their prey holds dear. They know that once you're hooked on the substance that you will do anything, including crime, to feed the addiction. They don't care about you because it's their way to a fast buck with all its temporary glitz.

Regardless of what you may think about Jesus, here's His judgment of such people upon which some modern law is based. "It is inevitable that stumbling blocks should come, but woe to him through whom they come! It would be better for him if a millstone were hung around his neck and he were thrown into the sea than that he should cause one of these little ones to stumble." Luke 17:1, 2. Resisting the stumbling blocks is a lifetime character building exercise. Students may as well start young by saying "no" to drugs.

Students who try a freebie drug just to see what it's like never plan to become addicts, but one exposure was enough to hook a friend of mine. For the next 19 years, he tried to conceal his drug dependence with lies and deceit, to the detriment of his relationship with his family and business associates. Even though he has been drug free for a decade and is now widely loved and respected, he will never cease being an addict in need of constant vigilance to keep from retrogressing. Such is the insidiousness of drugs.

According to my friend who has been drug free for 12 years, people who use drugs will in due course end up either dead, in jail, or, if they are lucky, in rehab. Consequently, one way or the other, the drug and its user will ultimately part company. Since it's not a question of if but rather of when the survivor decides to say "no," people who love themselves, their family and their friends will say no right up front and spare everybody the anguish brought about by drug abuse.

Otherwise, the next student zipped up in a body bag may be you.

Generational Chasm

This essay first appeared in The Dallas Morning News *on September 17, 2006.*

A generation gap has existed in the United States since the 1960s, when the term first characterized the cultural differences between post-World War II children and their elders. But I have been more than surprised numerous times to learn that the gap apparently has become a chasm.

While I was signing my book *Nine Years in the Saddle* at a local bookstore, a young high school English teacher (and aspiring author) stopped at my table and visited a while. My book is a true story that explicitly reveals how people on the ranches of the Great Southwest dealt with the Great Depression years from 1930 to 1939. Our conversation naturally included comments about that era.

So I asked this lady what she learned about the Great Depression in high school. Here's her reply: "Well, uh...everybody was poor...umm, there was a dust bowl in Oklahoma, and...umm, everybody was poor..." Responses similar to this at book signings all across the United States indicate that this void in 70-year-old history is not unique to North Texas. Some of the more knowledgeable respondents also know that the stock market crashed and that there were gangsters in Chicago.

Since schools use cross-curriculum teaching

techniques, I never expected to get such a response from any high school teacher. If teachers' knowledge of their grandparents' history is so limited, it should surprise no one that school tests reveal that some students think Nazi Germany was an ally of the United States in World War II.

This chasm in modern history is not new. In 1964, I entered a downtown office in Dallas, where two young ladies asked me to settle an argument for them. One thought that the term "battle of the bulge" was just a weight-loss term, while the other was sure that a real Battle of the Bulge had taken place but did not know where, when or the identity of the combatants. That was saddening and a bit shocking to this WWII vet, who had lost some comrades in that war, which had ended less than 20 years earlier.

George Santayana's oft-quoted statement that "those who cannot learn from history are doomed to repeat it" has become both a proverb and cliché. Yet its truth is as fresh as the sunrise.

Having spent some years teaching history in high schools, I'm aware of the challenge to make the subject come alive sufficiently to attract and retain the students' interest. That's understandable and may even be pardonable, if we are talking about such events as the rise of the Grecian empire under Alexander the Great or the significance of the Battle of Hastings. This is teacher territory. And not all teachers are charismatic, and, often, they lack parental support. This isn't news to anybody.

But why do the parents, grandparents and other older relatives seemingly fail to inculcate into the minds of their offspring the significant world events that shaped their own lives?

I don't know who dropped the ball for the young English teacher, but somebody did, and both she and the nation are the worse for it. A cursory examination of book titles in major bookstores suggests a high interest in memoirs. No one need be a published author to pass on family memoirs. From time to time, families have reunions at Thanksgiving, Christmas, or other designated times to assemble. What an excellent opportunity for the older folks to add significantly to the knowledge of the youngsters—and to the strength of the nation.

Unnecessarily Shot

It's still August, but I saw a sign in a supermarket advertising flu shots. This August announcement seems premature. According to the pharmaceutical companies, the medical establishment, the news media, and other interested parties, the flu virus usually shows up about October 1 each year. Isn't it interesting that the flu shots are available before the powers-that-be have decided what strain of flu virus they're promoting this year? The upcoming virus has no name yet, such as the bird flu, which came to nothing, or other viruses that didn't live up to their billing either.

I've never had a flu shot nor have I ever had the flu. Some years ago, I began to ponder some questions about all the hype about flu shots. Since those who promote the vaccine declare a "flu season" beginning in early fall, where do the viruses hang out the rest of the year? Usually, we are told there are multiple strains of viruses. How do the pharmaceutical companies know which strain needs a vaccine? And how do they manage to have most of the vaccine on hand at the precise time that the flu strain is identified?

Since those questions didn't have logical answers, I concluded that flu viruses were present all year. If so, why did people become more vulnerable in the fall and winter months and create what might appear to be an epidemic? So I did some investigation on the internet and discovered the obvious. The earth does not receive as much sunshine in the fall and winter months as it does the rest of the year, and what it does receive is not as intense. In addition, people stay indoors because of cold weather and receive little exposure to the sun, which is the source of vitamin D. Although some foods are fortified with small amounts of vitamin D, the only source of vitamin D3 is sunshine—or a food supplement. The fact that I was a long-time user of a multiple vitamin/mineral supplement containing D3 explained why I never got the flu.

Enlightened medical personnel recognize that vitamin D3 protects against flu viruses, and vitamin D is cheap. So why isn't it a general practice for doctors and the pharmaceutical companies with their retail outlets to recommend vitamin D instead of flu shots? Good question. The United States has about 300 million people. At $25 per flu shot, that's a potential market value of more than $7 billion. Consequently, the folks profiting from flu shots are not going to go quietly.

Poverty

Americans probably are the most generous people on earth. We not only rush to aid people in distress in our own communities, but are also first-responders to catastrophes wherever they occur in the world—often in countries whose governments are hostile to ours.

Unfortunately, humanitarian aid can be corrupted as easily as any other human endeavor. Who hasn't seen the photos of starving children with bloated bellies used as an appeal for your money, which will end up in the hands of scam artists? I had a tenderhearted friend who responded to such an appeal to "adopt" a needy child in Mexico. Although Black, he speaks Spanish fluently and told the agency that he had friends in Mexico and when he visited them, he wanted to stop by and meet his "adopted" child. That message ended all further contact.

I've been listening to politicians campaign on the poverty issue since W. Lee O'Daniel ran for governor of Texas in 1938. Yet solutions to poverty appear to be as intractable now, if not more so, than they were in 1938. Jesus was correct in saying that "...the poor you have with you always." But one of the obvious results of politicizing poverty is that many politicians have become rich and famous, while millions of ordinary people have found good jobs in charitable organizations—all compensated by taxation or willing donors.

Countless legitimate organizations with endless appeals exist to deal with various human frailties. Nobody can respond to all of them. Furthermore, once in place, some of these organizations do not disband when they complete their missions. For example, the March of Dimes was founded in 1938 to raise money for polio research. When the polio vaccine became available in 1955, the organization did not disband. It shifted its mission to preventing premature births and birth defects. This observation is not intended to denigrate the new cause, but to demonstrate how such causes mushroom and overwhelm donors. For some people, making money is easier than giving it away intelligently.

Although some kind of philanthropic organization covers most any human need in the United States, some in need still fall through the corporate cracks. Thoughtful donors do not give all they can to organizations so they can help such people individuality as opportunity presents itself.

And therein lies a challenge to good judgment. In effect such a person is asking, "What are you going to do about my problem?" My answer? "Nothing, unless you demonstrate that you are doing all you can to solve your own problem." Sad experience has taught me that it's impossible to help people who can, but won't, help themselves. My second caveat states that it is impossible to get a person out of a slum unless you also get the slum out of the person. Otherwise, all you will do is relocate the slum.

I've been to some Third World countries and seen people who would gladly accept the lifestyle of many of our people in poverty. That's why some risk their lives to come to the United States. That's also one reason that American churches send medical missionaries abroad. For multiple reasons, world-wide poverty will never be eradicated, but compassionate Americans do try to diminish it. Whether intended or not, poverty in other people tests the character of those of us who live above it.

A Poor Family in a Foreign Country

Compliments

Consider the goodwill you can get out of a simple compliment. While running across the campus when I was in college, I fell and skinned a leg sufficiently to justify a trip to the school nurse. While patching me up, she told me I had pretty legs. I had never associated the word pretty with any part of a man's anatomy—especially legs. Some women have pretty legs, but men's legs are simply functional.

I seldom bare my legs in public any more, but for a half century they had public exposure on more than fifty beaches around the world and several lakes where I water skied. And no other person ever commented on the quality of my legs. Yet occasionally, when I step out the shower and look in the mirror, I indulge myself the whimsy, "Hey man, you've got good looking legs." Such is the influence of one remembered compliment. The nurse's observation wasn't the inception of my life-long devotion to physical fitness. Nevertheless, her esteem gave it an imperceptible nudge. She also created in me a fond remembrance of her. That's what compliments do.

Since compliments bless both the giver and receiver, why do we ever withhold them? "It's more blessed to give than receive." No logical reason exists for doing so, but the excuse seems to lie in indifference and pride.

Pride is the barrier to many compliments since it's anchored in demands for its own recognition and is blind to excellence located elsewhere. Pride needs no accomplishments in wealth, power, or social status. It lurks in disdain. Abraham Lincoln is credited with saying that God must love the common man because he made so many of them. In his book *Generation of Vipers*, Philip Wiley countered that God must hate the common man because he made them so common. But if people are common, they made themselves that way. God creates unique masterpieces. Spreading around a few compliments may awaken some people to that potential.

Much of the time we're probably just oblivious to that which is complimentary in other people. It doesn't have to be that way. Simple awareness is the key. A few sincere compliments would put an end to a considerable amount of anger, pouting, and all the other insidious habits that alienate family members we are supposed to love.

Opportunities to compliment flourish everywhere. The next time you see a couple of policemen or highway patrolmen in a cafeteria, stop by and thank them for their service. Then to prove your sincerity, pick up their tabs. Other public servants merit equal treatment—especially garbage pick-up men and women who probably do more to maintain the health of the nation than all the medical personnel combined. Thanks to sanitation we haven't seen any Black Plagues lately.

We can demonstrate an unspoken compliment by showing patience and thoughtfulness for some fresh-faced youth with his foot on the first rung of the economic ladder, or an older person learning a new job out of necessity. They need all the encouragement they can get, and you can make their day—and yours.

A compliment and a smile have this in common: neither costs the giver anything, but both are priceless to the receiver—especially when given together.

Be Good; Be Responsible

When I was a child, the last thing I heard my mother say whenever I left the house to go anywhere was, "Be a good boy, Jamie." Although I had not analyzed the word "good," I knew exactly what she expected of me. My mother's concept of good was embedded in Christian principles taught by Jesus, the summation of which is found in the Golden Rule: "Do unto others as you would have them do unto you."

My step-father entered my life when I was age nine, and his frequent admonition was, "Take care of your money." I never got an allowance and one way or another had to earn whatever money I did have. During those Great Depression years, money was not easy to come by on the Plains of West Texas, and Dad meant for me to use money responsibly. He also taught me that money came about by the responsible use of my time. And whenever I hired out my services to work for another farmer, my dad reminded me that it was my responsibility to perform exactly as I was being paid to do whether or not I agreed with the farmer's instructions, which might deviate from the way I was accustomed to doing things on our own farm.

Neither of these people ever made it into high school, but if you had to come up with a five-word formula for successful living, I think you would be hard pressed to improve upon "Be good and be responsible."

I haven't always been good, nor have I always been responsible. But they set the standard for me, and if I missed it, the fault was mine.

Auther and Rita Reed, Parents of James V. Lee, Circa 1945